# GOD GOES TO COLLEGE

Greg - Congratulations &
Blessings on your new
adventures!

With love,
from your Youth Christian
Ed. committee

D1636156

# GOD GOES TO COLLEGE

## LIVING FAITH ON CAMPUS

Thomas C. Ettinger & Helen R. Neinast

UPPER
ROOM BOOKS®
NASHVILLE

Cover design: Christa Schoenbrodt
Cover image: Emanuele Taroni/Getty Images
Second printing: 2003

LIBRARY OF CONGRESS CATALOGING-IN-PUBLICATION DATA
Ettinger, Thomas C.
   God goes to college: living faith on campus / Thomas C. Ettinger,
Helen R. Neinast
      p. cm.
   ISBN: 0-8358-0987-0
  1. Christian college students—Religious life. I. Neinast, Helen R.
II. Title.
   BV4531.3 N45 2003
   248.8'34—dc21                               2002013577

Printed in the United States of America

# CONTENTS

FAITHFUL RELATIONSHIPS: KEEPING GOD AT THE CENTER

*This book is for*

*Wally Benson*
*Koty Copeland*
*Maddy Flores*
*Christopher Kammerer*
*Anna and Josh Kurtz*
*Cameron and Andrea Lovell*
*Yoki and Sam Moody-Wong*
*Katherine and Anna Nelson-Daniel*
*Jason, Aleighsha, Jaityn, and Valrie Stover*
*Nikki Taylor*

*who will themselves soon be storming the gates*
*of higher education*

# Introduction

God goes to college? But God knows everything. Why would God go to college? It's simple. God goes to college because that's where you are.

Some days you may feel that God is as far away from you as the home you left hundreds of miles away to come to college or the home you leave each day for the commute to campus.

But God is there. At college.

You just have to look. Maybe in some unexpected places. Maybe in some unexpected ways. And amid some pretty unexpected situations.

But God is there, searching for you even as you search for God. *God Goes to College: Living Faith on Campus* is meant to be a companion for you during your college years. All along the way—in good times and bad—this book can help you strengthen your faith, your witness, and your relationship with God.

Use this book to deepen your spiritual life. Use it as a guide for prayer and reflection that will support you in your growth as a Christian and as a student. Use it for your personal devotional time or use it with a study group. Read an essay; take some time to reflect on what you've read; then, take time to listen—to God and to yourself. In the process you just might find courage, grace, compassion, and strength you didn't know you had.

And remember: God does go to college—right alongside you, every step of the way.

### A Word about Us

God's been going to college for years. We know that's true from experience—God was an important part of our own college years. Tom went to St. Petersburg Community College and the University of South Florida. Helen graduated from McMurry University in Texas. We met at Duke University Divinity School where both of us were students.

And God has been there with us all along.

We are both ordained ministers who have worked with college students in local churches and on campuses. Tom spent time in ministry in Florida, and Helen worked in New Mexico. Helen has also worked with a national church agency on higher education and ministry, and Tom has been a counselor in private practice. From 1994 until 2002, we shared the United Methodist campus ministry at Emory University in Atlanta, Georgia.

We married in 1990 and live in the mountains of northeast Georgia with our dog, Maggie, and our two cats, Jake and Kate.

# BEING A STUDENT

## God's Call and Vision For You

# VOCATIONS, CAREERS, AND CALLINGS
## REFLECTIONS ON YOUR WORK

You've heard it said before. It may have been your parents, your professors, or a Pepsi commercial, but you've heard it: You are the next generation. The next generation of leaders.

Though you've heard that you are the next generation before, try to hear it again—this time in a new way. Hear it as a call from God; hear it as a call to find your vocation; hear it as a call to meet the world at its leading edge.

For you, college is a time to explore, to listen, to dream, to hear the call to vocation. In these weeks and months and years you can awaken to who you are and to what you are called to do.

The call to vocation is for you not unlike the Israelites' call as they stood at the edge of the Red Sea. They faced a moment of decision, hearing Moses' call to follow to the water's edge as it parted and Miriam's call of celebration on the other side, beckoning them on to the Promised Land. The call to vocation is for you not unlike the call the disciples heard when Jesus said, "If any want to become my followers, let them deny themselves and take up their cross and follow me" (Matt. 16:24).

As you struggle to figure out your call to vocation, remember that Jesus also struggled with his. He had to discover who he was in relationship to God and what it was that God intended him to do. The Holy Spirit led him on his vocational quest.

At Jesus' baptism, the Holy Spirit revealed that Jesus was the Son of God. Then Jesus was led into the wilderness to wrestle with what that reality meant in the work he was to do. After Jesus left the wilderness to follow his vocation, the people of God did not always affirm his calling. In Luke 4, after Jesus' first public speech at the temple, his hearers were "filled with rage." They rose up and ran him out of town.

Even at the end of his life, Jesus struggled to understand his calling. His deep uncertainty at the garden of Gethsemane just before his betrayal and death reveals that even then he struggled to listen for God's call.

God has, in some way or another, called you to the place you are right here, right now. May it be for you a holy place, a joyful place, a place to explore, to play, to risk, to act, and to grow.

May it be for you, most of all, a place to listen . . . to listen for the call of God. You never know what you might discover.

# LOVING GOD WITH YOUR MIND
## The Sacredness of Study

∼

The life of the mind. A college professor I had in my first year of college used to talk about "the life of the mind" every year when classes began.

At the time, the phrase evoked images of a science fiction movie for me: "Who knows what lurks in the life of the mind?" Pretty scary stuff to my already overstimulated first-week-in-college imagination.

Later on that year, and over the course of the next three, I began to get a glimmer of what my professor was talking about. While I sat in the library late one night, struggling over a complex programming exercise, the wonders of the computer's language suddenly came clear. Staring at a math problem, I saw the solution crystallize on the page. Insight emerged into the workings of one particular poem by e.e.

cummings. The questions of the history professor compelled me to search for new answers, new notions, new ideas.

So that's what my professor meant: the life of the mind. Learning gives way to insight, and insight gives birth to joy and wonder, discipline, imagination.

Your life's work at present, your vocation right now, is to be a student. To study, to learn, to question, to challenge, to imagine, to stretch the limits of knowledge. The exercise of the mind, the vision of the mind's eye—these surely are holy ways to love God. Your studies will raise questions and doubts. Jesus welcomed questions and doubts in his followers.

Revel in your studies, even when they threaten to overwhelm you. Consecrate your desk, even when you don't want to spend time there. Make your textbooks holy vessels. Confess ignorance, receive God's invitation to learn, use the power of your imagination. Love God with your mind.

# STUDY
## A Holy Vocation

In his book *The Centering Moment*, Howard Thurman offers a wonderful prayer for the students of the world. He asks that all students be held "steadily, quietly, with great concentration before Thy altar."

I came across this prayer during my first year in graduate school, and I kept a copy of it on my desk at home. Only after several weeks of using this prayer each time I sat down to study did it occur to me what Thurman must have meant by "Thy altar." I realized this prayer was calling me not to a traditional altar in a church but was suggesting I consider my desk as God's altar—the altar upon which I made my daily offering of study.

That image brought me up short. To consider my studies as an offering to God gave new meaning and vitality to my work as a student. To be sure, there were days when my studies intrigued me, when the books I read inspired me, and when I felt the papers I wrote were insightful. But there were other days when my study was grudging, my mind dull, and my papers labored.

Using Thurman's image of my desk as an altar reminded me in a powerful way that all my study time—inspired or boring, insightful or labored—belonged to God. It meant that as I studied I was blessing God. That prayer vividly reminded me that my vocation as student was a sacred vocation.

As you approach your studies, remind yourself that God has called you at this time in your life to the vocation of student. As you approach your desk or your study carrel or the library, remind yourself that you are approaching God's altar. Offer your studies up to God with thanksgiving for the gift of learning.

# Choosing Majors and Careers
## Listening for a Calling

"What's your major?" That's the college version of "What do you want to be when you grow up?" If you've been asked the question once, you've probably been asked it a hundred times. How you answer it depends entirely on the circumstances in which you find yourself at any one particular time.

Some students decide early on exactly what their field of study will be, and they never veer from that initial course. Others major in "undecided" as long as possible, choose a major only when forced to by school policy, and then change majors two or three times before they graduate.

Some people know the career they want to pursue from the time they're ten years old. Others go through the traditional childhood litany of vocations—firefighter, doctor, teacher, astronaut, actor—and end up in college still unsure of what they want to do with their work lives.

No matter which category fits you, here are some things to think about:

- *Vocation* comes from a Latin word that means "calling," and that's exactly what vocations are: callings to use your gifts and talents in the world. Prayerfully consider where God's call is guiding and directing you.

- Your choice of vocation affects your life powerfully—not just financially but psychologically, emotionally, and spiritually. Yet your life is much more than just your work. Seek balance between your work life and your life away from work.

- Gathering information about career opportunities, that is, "doing your homework," is essential. It can be hard work, but stick with it.

- Change of job or career does not equal failure. In fact, changing careers often turns out to be a process of "fine tuning," of coming closer to where you need to be. Disappointment, even failure, can put you on the path toward the vocation that fits you best.

- Very little drains the spirit more than being in a vocation you do not like or you don't feel called to. Pay attention to how you feel about what you're studying in your major courses. Those feelings will give you clues about the work you need to be moving toward.

- Everyone has a vocational calling. For some, that calling may be to work professionally in the church. For others, that calling may be to work in the secular world. Either way, your vocation is a sacred calling.

"What's your major?" "What do you want to be when you grow up?" Even though we're both many years out of college, we still sometimes wonder about those questions. As we wrestle with our callings, we remind ourselves that God's grace sustains us amidst our questions. As you wrestle with your calling, remind yourself of that promise too.

# MAKING THE GRADE
## Measuring Up

The tyranny of grades, of making it, of doing well. Sometimes, in academia as well as in football, it turns out that winning isn't everything—it's the *only* thing.

The examples of fallout from the pressure to succeed are rampant. Someone steals a copy of the test used to accredit physicians. A famous historian is uncovered as a plagiarist. The honor board at a prestigious university expels a dozen students for cheating on final exams. The number of suicides among young people—many at least partially the result of academic pressure—is alarmingly high and growing.

The pressure to make the grade, to make the team, to make it into the finals is very real. It's one way—an insidious way—of measuring yourself against others.

Don't get the wrong impression. Grades are important,

but so is learning on the way to getting the grade. Doing your best is important, but so is not doing yourself in as you strive for your best.

So, in addition to grades, fraternity or sorority membership, and where you finish in the triathlon, you'd better come up with some other ways to measure yourself, to keep track of your studies, to define who you are.

Grace is another way to measure yourself. The measure of God's grace is lavished upon you, according to the Gospel of John (see 1:16). Because you are a child of God, you are accepted and loved—that is God's grace and that is the real measure of who you are.

When you have done your best, when you have run the race as well as you can, God's grace meets you, takes your measure, and finds that you are God's own—beloved, holy, God's son or daughter. A member of the family of God.

So whether you're concerned about grades or athletics or relationships, let God's grace give you the courage to live life fully. Don't be afraid to venture out, to stretch yourself, to follow your imagination. Sure, you're still human, and at some point in the future, failure and limitation will visit you without warning. You cannot deny that inevitability. But these things—failure and limitations—are not the ultimate measures of life. Grace is the ultimate measure. Grace. Pure and simple.

# YOU ARE NOT YOUR G.P.A.

Have you ever had a teacher or professor who taught you as much about life outside the classroom as he or she taught you about the subject area inside the classroom? I was fortunate enough to have two such professors in my life: Ellen Hoffman and Carlyle Marney. Both are now dead. They never met. But they would have liked each other, because they shared some basic convictions about education.

Hoffman was my undergraduate government professor. She loved things political. For many years, she worked on staff for a U.S. senator. She reveled in the study of government. She had an infectious laugh, a welcoming spirit, and a keen mind.

Marney, one of my preaching professors in graduate school, was a crusty, down-to-earth Southern Baptist minister who liked to say, "Those who ordained me would take it back if they could." After a significant pause for effect he'd add with glee, "But they can't."

Marney loved being able to integrate different academic disciplines. It thrilled him to help others see the interconnectedness of their various studies. Most of all, he loved caring for and teaching other pastors.

Each of these professors gave me important insights into the world of grades and learning. Hoffman, who had adopted two baby girls, once told me, "In the twenty-five years since I finished graduate school, no one has ever asked me what my grade point average was. And I've decided that as long as my daughters give a good effort at learning, their grades will take care of themselves. I want them to enjoy their years in college, not to be in constant turmoil, trying to do everything perfectly."

Marney told all his final-semester theology students this about the degree we were about to receive: "Your degree won't be worth a plug nickel in five years if you don't use what you have learned here. No matter what your grades are, if you haven't learned how to ask questions and search for the answers, your degree will be worthless. Knowing how to ask questions, knowing how to study, being willing and able to search for the resources to answer your questions—these are the keys to judging your degree."

You see, Ellen Hoffman and Carlyle Marney understood that learning involved much more than exam scores and grade point averages. They understood that God speaks a great word of grace to all who would hear it. To sum up their advice: Give college a good effort. Let the grades take care of themselves. Have fun. Learn now how to find the resources you will need after you graduate. Let go of your anxiety about grades and discover the joy of learning. It's all part of loving God with your mind.

T.C.E.

# THE HOLINESS OF TIME
## A Faith Perspective on Time Management

Ben Franklin knew it: "Time is money." Chaucer wrote about it: "Time lost may not recovered be." Eugene Ionesco put it succinctly: "We haven't the time to take our time."

As a college student, you have no doubt discovered the dilemma of time. You have to balance the time demands placed on your day by family, friends, extracurricular activities, studies, and roommates. College students engage in "time wars," battling the clock to organize, reorganize, spend, and save time.

Dozens of books, philosophies, advice givers, workshops, and organizers can help you manage your time. Day-Runners, Day-Timers, Palm Pilots . . . the list of tools goes on and on.

Odette Lockwood-Stewart, while serving as a campus minister, asked two questions at the heart of our relationship with time: "What do we do with the time we save through hurry, technology, schedules, and clever calendars? . . . What might our calendars and date books reveal about the meaning of the book our days are writing?"

Categories like "sacred" and "secular" simply do not apply to the minutes, hours, and days of our lives. Morning and night, work time and play—it is all sacred.

In the middle of your hectic schedule, remember that. All time is holy . . . and, because of that fact, to manage and to care for your time is a holy act. Don't let the urgent things crowd out the important ones. Take time, each day, to discern the difference between the two.

# STUDYING THE BIBLE

Imagine using the Bible to justify trapping human beings, stacking them in the cargo holds of ships, sailing them three thousand miles across a great ocean, stripping them naked, placing them on an auction block, and selling them into a lifetime of slavery. It happened—and not so very long ago.

People have used the Bible to justify bans on playing cards, going to movies, touring art museums, using makeup, wearing shorts. One rationalization is that these activities aren't in the Bible so people shouldn't do them. (One wonders how such folks regard the nonbiblical flush toilet!)

Some people use the Bible to deny others their civil rights; some use it to avoid the discipline of medical and scientific models of discovery, understanding, and knowledge.

These are extreme examples of abusing the Bible, yet none of us is immune from this kind of misuse. Interpreting the Bible requires a careful approach. First, approach the Bible in a spirit of discovery—learning about God through Jesus and the Hebrew scriptures, allowing growth to take place through God's grace, increasing your capacity to love. If this is not your approach, your interpretation will likely be focused on manipulation, exploitation, and power politics.

Second, when you seek to interpret what you read in the Bible (and interpret you must), you have to decide what to take literally and what to take symbolically. You have to use your mind—the logical part of you—to understand what certain teachings mean.

Some cases in point: In Revelation, the great apocalyptic dragon knocks stars out of the sky with its tail (Rev. 12:4). Symbol or a ten-billion-mile-long dragon? What about Jesus' statement, "If your right eye causes you to sin, tear it out" (Matt. 5:29)? Is he speaking figuratively, or should we all go out and buy eye patches?

The Hebrew scripture calls for "an eye for eye, tooth for tooth" (Exod. 21:24). If you take the scripture literally, what should you do if a blind guy with dentures hits you? As Tevye in *Fiddler on the Roof* observes, if that scripture is taken literally, the whole world would end up blind and toothless.

When Jesus says, "If any want to become my followers, let them deny themselves and take up their cross and follow me" (Matt. 16:24), is he calling for us literally to be crucified, or is he calling us to be prepared to make sacrifices in our lives? It matters very much whether you approach the Bible literally or symbolically.

Finally, when you seek God through the Bible, you must be prepared to be changed. The Bible has the power to meet you where you are in your faith journey and to move you along—sometimes slowly, one step at a time, and sometimes with amazing speed. Approach the Bible with eagerness and openness, and God will meet you there. Seek to be changed by God's Word, and you will be guided along the way.

# UNDERSTANDING GOD'S WILL
## FOR YOUR LIFE

I've studied for this test all I'm going to. If I fail the course, it's God's will."

"He was so young. But God called him home. His death must be God's will."

"If I only knew God's will for my life, I could concentrate better on my studies."

Lots of things—good and bad—get attributed to God as God's will. It's tough sometimes to know when and how God is acting in the world. And how do you tell when something is God's will and when it is just your own will? It's confusing.

Little Katie, a child in my church, was so alive, so full of energy before she got sick. A wonderful kid. Yet she contracted leukemia at the tender age of three. Why her? Why anyone?

As the illness progressed, it became impossible to count all those who joined in the fight to help Katie. I watched the hospital staff care so much—hating the pain of the treatments even as they inflicted them. I watched simple people, those whom Jesus called the salt of the earth, increase their saltiness even as they suffered along with Katie's family. They said prayers, expressed doubt, prayed in faith, hoped against hope, and loved unceasingly.

When I consider all that happened during those three years—the calls, cards, food, donations, visits, and prayers on behalf of Katie—I know that I am closer to understanding God's will. As Dorothee Soelle has pointed out, the issue is "not 'where does the tragedy come from?' but 'where does it lead?'" God calls each of us to use our heart, mind, soul, and strength to learn, to care, to love, and, yes, to cure disease. God has given us all we need to do these very things.

The battle against leukemia goes on. Yet this particular battle for Katie's life is over. She died at the age of six. It is yet another mystery, this time a sad one.

God's will does make itself known—in the actions of people, in the words of the Bible, and through your own reason and experience. As you seek to do God's will—to love

God with your whole being and to love your neighbor as yourself—you may not find answers to all your questions; but you will, day by day, learn to discern the will of God—both for your life and for the life of the world.

# THE NOBLE ART OF LEAVING THINGS UNDONE

Even God rested—it says so in the Bible. Farmers let fields lie fallow from time to time. The school year is divided into terms, with winter and summer breaks. Major league baseball takes a midseason three-day All-Star break. And the industrious ant returns to its cool, dark underground home each evening.

Not so for us. We live with—demand, actually—twenty-four-hour stores, day-and-night automatic banking, and the relentless speed of the Internet.

"The three great American vices," says Chinese scholar Lin Yutang in *The Importance of Living*, "seem to be efficiency, punctuality and the desire for achievement and success. They are the things that make the Americans so unhappy and so nervous." He goes on to speak about the inalienable right to loaf, the noble art of getting things done, and the nobler art of leaving things undone.

Jesus, who was much in demand and besieged by a great number of people, managed to hold in balance his mission with his need for rest. First, he taught multitudes, and he also met those in need one person at a time. But then he went away by himself, prayed, spent time in quiet, and rested.

Given Christ's example, try something different. Do nothing. For fifteen minutes one day, simply do nothing. Leave something undone and do nothing. If you catch yourself starting to do something, put it away and go back to doing nothing. Sometimes it's time to "do nothing" for God.

# LIVING YOUR FAITH EACH DAY

Some Essentials

# FINDING GOD AMID THE NOISE AND PRESSURE

We seem to be running all the time. The notion of settling into a quiet place and being reflective is a good one—an important one—but some days life just doesn't happen that way.

Sometimes the noise and the pressure don't—or won't—go away, even for a little while. Take the whole idea of observing Advent in the middle of final exams and papers. Amid all that pressure, how do you find time for God? Or take the living arrangement at college—whether your parents' home, a dorm room, or a shared apartment—it's not exactly a prayer sanctuary! In the middle of all that noise, how do you find space for God?

Oddly enough, the only place to find God in the middle of all the noise and pressure is just that—in the middle of all the noise and pressure. And if life's hectic pace catches you sometimes out of breath, slow up a little, breathe a little deeper, and let your breath become a prayer to God.

Sometimes God's peace and serenity will elude you. Sometimes you will elude the peace and serenity God offers. When that happens, remember that God is, somehow, still there in the middle of it all.

# Finding God in Solitude and Quiet

"Inside yourself, you shouldn't be running all the time." That's Tina Turner, rock superstar, quoting a Trappist monk. Turner, a practicing Buddhist, and the monk, a practicing Catholic, have a basic belief in common: It takes time and solitude and a sense of quiet in order to know God.

"Be still, and know that I am God!" A simple verse from the Bible, yet it is one of the hardest to follow. When was the last time you sat still—perfectly still—for any length of time? Not just your body but your mind. It's harder than it sounds and more rewarding than you can imagine.

God reaches out to each of us all the time—through other people and through circumstance and in that "still small voice." Most of the time, though, we're so busy, so active, so preoccupied that we don't hear what God is trying to say.

Quiet and solitude are such important parts of the life of faith because God waits for you in the silence and solitude. The more often you practice solitude, the more often you will find the God who waits, and the more often you will hear the God who speaks.

To quiet the body, to quiet the mind, to sit still and do nothing. These are important things. Author Robert Fulghum senses the power of sitting still. In fact, he humorously suggests that a new religion could be based on this act. To belong would simply require sitting still for fifteen minutes a day. "Amazing things might happen if enough people did this on a regular basis," he says. "Every chair, park bench, and sofa would become a church."

Quiet the body. Quiet the mind. Be still. Amazing things might happen. Just try it and see.

# THE PRACTICE OF PRAYER
## Beating a Path to God's Door

Frederick Buechner says that everybody prays, whether he or she thinks of it as prayer or not. Buechner believes that prayer makes itself known in all sorts of forms—the silence that comes when you confront something amazing and wonderful, the pain you feel when someone you love hurts, the angry cry when someone hurts you, the hope rising in your heart when you hear news that is too good not to be true.

Lots of people have written lots of books about the practice of prayer. Prayer as listening to God. Prayer as talking to God. Prayer as adoration, confession, thanksgiving, supplication. Prayer as the silence that comes with a deep peace. Prayer that cries out loud to God in anguish. Prayer that slowly, ever so slowly, changes the heart of the one who prays.

According to the Bible, the most important thing to remember about prayer is to keep at it. In Luke Jesus tells two stories about the practice of prayer. In one he compares prayer to knocking on a friend's door at midnight to borrow bread—knocking and knocking until the sleepy friend finally gets up and gives you the bread you're asking for. In another story, Jesus says the practice of prayer is like approaching the crooked judge who doesn't want to hear the poor widow's case but finally does simply because of her persistence.

Whatever else prayer is—petition, confession, thanksgiving, or silence shared between you and God—the Bible says to practice it over and over and over again. For it is in the practice of prayer that you seek God and God seeks you.

Practice prayer. Keep at it. No matter what. Even when the answers you get are not the ones you expected or prayed for, remember this: Prayer is beating a path to God's door and allowing God to beat a path to yours.

# PRACTICING PRAYER
## ON THE LEVEL

When reporters want to get past the "official story" to something closer to the truth, they often ask: "What can you tell me, strictly off the record?"

Strictly off the record. In confidence. Just between you and me. Not to be repeated. Things said quietly in private that are a step closer to the truth than things said out loud in public. That's what it's like to practice prayer on the level. You cut through the first layers of the truth in order to get to the bare bones. You "level" with God and with yourself. You speak the truth about your thoughts, your feelings, your deeds, your desires.

Whether the truth you share is good news or bad news, glorious or unspeakable, God is already there to receive you—all of you—in prayer. And when you give yourself fully and honestly, opening to God in prayer, the promise is sure and true and trustworthy. You are accepted by God, healed, loved.

Don't be afraid to practice prayer on the level. God will meet you wherever, however, whoever you are in the moment.

# Practicing Prayer
# on the Run

Almost every letter Paul wrote in the New Testament begins and ends with a word of grace. Most of his letters begin with a prayer of thanksgiving and a promise of constant prayer for those to whom he writes.

Hebrews 13:15 tells us to "continually" offer God "a sacrifice of praise," and 1 Thessalonians 5:17 says we should "pray without ceasing." Romans 12:12 urges us to "persevere in prayer." Ephesians 6 counsels us to "pray in the Spirit at all times."

In the Bible, believers pray in prison, on a ship in the middle of a storm, in solitary places, alone, and in the middle of the busyness of the day.

Your days as a student will be full, rushed, overflowing with too much to do. The "busyness of the day" may well be the only time you have available for prayer. As you rush from one class to another, from one club meeting to the next study session, devote your hurriedness to God. This, in itself, is a form of prayer.

Mark reports that Jesus often prayed at night (Mark 1:35; 6:46, 48). This was his time, the time, as Howard Thurman puts it, "for the long breath . . . when voices that had been quieted by the long day's work could once more be heard." Yet Jesus too understood what it meant to pray constantly, throughout the day.

For Jesus, as for all believers, God breathes through all that is—through all the important, insignificant, joyous, and frightening things that happen in the course of a day. To be aware of God's presence in your life every day, all day, is to be practicing prayer even when you are on the run.

# RITUAL, SYMBOL, AND SACRAMENT

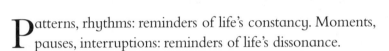

Patterns, rhythms: reminders of life's constancy. Moments, pauses, interruptions: reminders of life's dissonance.

Rituals mark ceremonies, graduations, celebrations, memorial services, prayers at mealtimes, the nightly routine of going to bed, and the daily routine of getting up.

"From beginning to end," writes Robert Fulghum in *From Beginning to End*, "the rituals of our lives shape each hour, day, and year. Everyone leads a ritualized life. . . . If you are mindful of your actions, you will see the ritual patterns. If you see the patterns, you may understand them. If you understand them, you may enrich them. In this way, the habits of a lifetime become sacred."

Think about it. Your academic year is full of rituals—some for the beginning of term, some for midterm, others for the end of a year of study. Day to day, as a student, you have rituals too—how and when you study, how you get ready for an exam, what you do when it's time to research and write a paper. You have rituals with your friends at school—Friday-night trivia games, Saturday hikes and movies, Sunday evenings at the campus ministry center.

As creatures of rhythm, we, no less than the rest of creation, are captured by rituals: great ones and small ones, daily ones and once-in-a-lifetime ones. In many ways, our basic needs for living are extraordinarily simple, and they haven't changed much over the centuries. We eat, sleep, bathe, work. Understanding and creating rituals in these areas of life enrich our everyday lives and bind us to the sacred.

Jesus himself had a fine sense of ritual. In his teaching and in his daily life with his followers he blessed mealtimes and the beginning and ending of the day. He understood the power of the moment and honored it with a ritual. And his followers, to this day, have never forgotten him for it.

# THE POWER OF GRATITUDE

It comes between *gratis* (free, for nothing) and *gratuitous* (unearned) in the dictionary. It's what your parents made you say when someone gave something to you or did anything for you. And it's what you expressed in note after endless note for all the gifts you received at high school graduation.

*Gratitude.* Whether urged by parents, dictated by social custom, or spoken straight from the heart, gratitude is a powerful force. The *American Heritage Dictionary* defines gratitude as "an awareness," and that's precisely what it is. Gratitude is awareness of life as gift—all the big things and all the little things and all the things in between that are unearned, freely given. No charge to the receiver.

Though we sometimes forget to be grateful, it is easy to do when things in life go well—good weather, good marks on the exam, a good class schedule for winter term. When things don't go so well, gratitude is tougher.

And yet gratitude—in good circumstances or bad—offers great transformational power. To say thank you, to practice gratitude for life even with its pain, discomfort, and stress, is to recognize life for what it is—a gift from God. And this recognition, this awareness, is one of the most irresistible forces in the world, because it affirms life, it affirms the present, it puts you in right relationship with the world.

Jesus lived a life of practiced gratitude. He encouraged others to do the same. Let your faith encourage an awareness of life as gift in you. Be grateful. Say thank you. Practice gracious acceptance of life—all of it.

There will be times when gratitude is easy, when saying thank you comes naturally. There will be other times when you must force gratitude. Must say thank you. Must say thank you when you don't feel especially grateful. Eventually, the power of gratitude will take over, and a true awareness of life (in all its circumstances) as gift will begin.

# CONFESSION
## Bridging the Gap

Y ou'd better confess now. You don't want me to have to hear from somebody else what you've done. 'Cause if I hear it from someone else, you're gonna wish you'd told me the truth when I asked you."

That was my mother, confronting me and my two brothers when she knew—just by looking at our faces—that we were guilty of some childhood misbehavior. My mother subscribed to the old adage that confession is good for the soul. At the time, as a ten-year-old, I was quite sure she was wrong. How could confession be good if, when I did confess to something I'd done, I got sent to my room without supper? Confession might have been good for my soul, but I quickly figured out that it was not so good for my taste buds or my body.

Years later, as I became familiar with the Twelve Step recovery process, I heard echoes of my mother's adage in the program. More specifically I heard it stated in the Fifth Step: "Admitted to God, to ourselves and to another human being the exact nature of our wrongs."

That requirement struck me, on first hearing, as an extreme measure. It was bad enough to face up to my own shortcomings but to have to confess all that to God and to another human being? It seemed a bit much. After all, I rationalized, God already knew all my wrongs, and what human being would still want to associate with me after hearing "the exact nature" of what I'd done?

Then I came across Frederick Buechner's definition of confession, and some pieces began to fall into place. No, confessing your sins isn't telling God anything God doesn't already know; but, Buechner adds, "Until you confess them . . . they are the abyss between you. When you confess them, they become the bridge."

That idea intrigued me. Those things that most separate me from God could, by my confession of them, be changed into a bridge between us.

That was it—the key to confession and to why it is good for the soul. The great chasm of sin is crossed by the bridge of confession and forgiveness.

Not only is the chasm between God and me bridged by confession; the chasm between other people and me is also covered by that bridge. To say, "I'm sorry; please forgive me" to another person and to have that person forgive me is to close the gap between us.

Take a risk. Practice confession—between you and God, between you and other people. It is the bridge that spans the chasms of hurt, pain, and wrongdoing. It is the bridge that leads to peace.

# FORGIVENESS

F orget and forgive." Shakespeare said it in *King Lear*. Miguel de Cervantes echoed the advice in *Don Quixote*. Alexander Pope, an eighteenth-century writer, recognized the importance of forgiveness in "An Essay on Criticism." Dolores Huerta, a leader in the fight for the rights of migrant workers in the '60s and '70s, cited the power of forgiveness in the struggle for justice.

Poets, playwrights, authors, activists—these and many others throughout history—have struggled with the challenge of forgiveness. Jesus himself often taught his listeners this fundamental requirement and urged it upon them. Yet forgiveness remains a difficult task. After years of counseling with adults of all ages, I find that accepting forgiveness for oneself is also a tough hurdle in the healing process.

Time and again I discover people who cannot—will not—believe that the love of God in Christ reaches out to them across the centuries to accept them, just the way they are. If you are unable to accept Christ's forgiveness by refusing to forgive yourself, you effectively close the door between you and Christ. But Christ is persistent. He offers forgiveness and the chance to accept it again and again.

You may be having trouble forgiving yourself for something right now. Imagine that Jesus is standing at your door, wanting to love you in ways that will bring you forgiveness and newness of life. The door, however, has no outside handle. It can only be opened by you—from the inside. You have the choice to open the door, accept Christ's forgiveness, and be loved by Christ, just as you are.

Inability to accept God's loving forgiveness through Christ results in missed opportunities to become a new creature in Christ, to change and be changed. Welcome the love of Christ into your life. By offering forgiveness, God clears all the obstacles out of the way. Open the door and meet God on the cleared path by accepting that forgiveness for yourself. Then seek to forgive others as you have been forgiven.

# MAKING TIME FOR WORSHIP

Weekly worship marks time by making time to be part of a faith community. Most worship services still take place on Sunday mornings, but many churches offer Saturday evening services, midweek services, and daily Mass. Campus ministries often observe evening vespers or midnight prayer services on weekdays.

No matter *when* you go to worship, go to worship. Gathering with other Christians weekly for worship is one of the most crucial disciplines of the spiritual life.

We don't come to worship to find God. We come instead to be found by God. And God is intimately present in the community at worship.

Jewish law prefers that Jews pray together, and we Christians are heirs to that tradition. Joseph Telushkin, a leader of the National Jewish Center for Learning and Leadership (and author of the Rabbi Daniel Winter murder mysteries) suggests that the rabbis believed public prayers were more apt to be offered with the benefit of the entire community in mind. Individuals praying alone, they suspected, often prayed mostly for themselves.

Dan Wakefield, writing about his own spiritual journey, says he realized that going to church, even belonging to a church, did not solve his life's problems. Attending church did, however, give him a sense of being part of something greater than himself. He reported that it widened his view beyond the narrow lens of his own personal concerns.

In an interview shortly before his death, Henri Nouwen commented on his discovery that community worship was crucial for his prayer life. "I can do prayer best when I do it in the company of others," he said.

Don't let intramural sports or academic pressures or the hectic pace of your life as a student keep you from worship. Find a faith community that can nourish you, sustain you, challenge you, and feed your soul. Find a weekly worship place where God can find you.

# LAUGHTER
## Does God Have a Sense of Humor?

Bobby Bowden, head football coach at Florida State University, was asked once if he thought God had a sense of humor. "Does God have a sense of humor? Yeah, sure. Just turn around and take a look at the guy sitting next to you."

Does God have a sense of humor? Take a look at an aardvark, an anteater, or any of nature's creatures with long noses, necks, or knees. God *does* have a sense of humor.

It all starts in the Bible, of course. In Genesis 17, God tells Abraham, at the age of ninety-nine, that he and his ninety-year-old wife, Sarah, are going to have a baby. In the first version of the story, Abraham bursts out laughing in response to the news. In the next chapter, when the story is retold, it is Sarah who is overcome with laughter.

Faith sometimes is laughter and humor and absurdity all wrapped up into one. Isaiah tells the faithful, "With joy you will draw water from the wells of salvation" (Isa. 12:3). With joy.

In 1964 Norman Cousins was struck by a life-threatening illness. His doctors gave him a one-in-five-hundred chance of recovery. Determined to muster all the resources available to him, Cousins set out on an unconventional road to healing, one that included laughter as part of the treatment. "It worked. I made the joyous discovery that ten minutes of genuine belly laughter had an anesthetic effect and would give me at least two hours of pain-free sleep," he reports in his book *Anatomy of an Illness: As Perceived by the Patient.*

Our God laughs well and invites us to do so too.

# GOD'S EXTRAVAGANT GRACE
## Smoothing Out the Rough Edges

*Prevenient grace* is God meeting you at every corner. *Justifying grace* is reaching out to meet God's love, saying yes, and turning a corner in your faith journey. What comes next? Smoothing out the rough edges. The theologians call that *sanctification*, and it is a lifelong process, full of fits and starts along the way.

For John Wesley, God's smoothing grace, God's sanctifying grace, led believers to have hearts "habitually filled with the love of God and neighbor."

For you, grace might mean coming to understand your life as more and more focused on living by faith. Instead of dabbling in the faith, you come to understand the faith as the hub, the center out of which you live. Little by little, God's grace uncovers more of God's image in you. In this process a "new, improved version" of yourself emerges. You become better able to love God, neighbor, and yourself.

As a person forgiven, you become more forgiving. As a person who is loved, you become more loving. As a person healed, you start to become a healer.

The process is slow, sometimes painful, sometimes joyous, always moving just one day at a time. But once you fall in love, once you turn the corner, once you set out on the road to sanctification, God's extravagant grace promises you wonderful surprises along the way.

# Embracing Doubt

If you've ever been called a "doubting Thomas," you probably realize the title is not considered a compliment. Whoever used that phrase most likely meant to test you, embarrass you, or get your attention. Maybe that other person was exasperated with all your questions and simply wanted you to shut up. Or perhaps you yourself called someone else a "doubting Thomas" when her or his questions outweighed your answers.

"Doubting Thomas." The ultimate put-down. Or is it?

In *The Agony of Christianity*, Miguel de Unamuno defines a faith that has no doubts as a faith that is dead. Columnist Sydney J. Harris often comments that those with easy answers prove they don't know much about the scope of the questions they are asking. According to Isaac Bashevis

Singer, doubt is an important part of all religion. And Robert Browning contended that the more doubt you have, the stronger your faith.

Faith and doubt are not antagonists, according to Lillian Smith, campus ministry director with The United Methodist Church. Instead, she says, they work together side by side to strengthen faith. And contemporary author Margaret Drabble is convinced that when nothing is sure, it means anything and everything is possible.

Do you have doubts—about the faith, about life, about yourself? Good for you. As unsettling as those doubts may be, nurture them. Embrace them. Refine them. For it is only through doubt that faith and knowledge grow. Never fear the questions. Fear those who won't let you ask questions.

When Jesus went into the temple as a young boy, he asked his teachers many questions, and they were amazed, the Bible tells us. Amaze yourself. Follow in Jesus' footsteps. Be a doubting Thomas. Track down your questions and doubts and trust that God is pleased with your keen interest.

# HARD TIMES
## Mourning and Being Comforted

When my younger brother died, I remember how much I hurt inside. It felt as though there was a bloody hole where my heart should have been. After the sharp wrench of pain and shock fell away, I remember a dull, empty ache. And underneath the ache, I remember nothing at all—the numbness of death itself.

Friends came to me—to talk, to listen, to sit with me. I prayed, searched the Bible for words of comfort, got angry at God, wept, slept exhausted, and slept not at all.

I went back to my work; the dull ache and numbness went with me.

"Blessed are those who mourn. . . ." Jesus' words haunted me. The mourning part I was beginning to understand—how wrenching, how lonely, how terrifying it can be. Blessed?

That part rang hollow. I felt no blessing in the middle of the pain. For a long, long time I felt no blessing and no comfort.

Then slowly, imperceptibly, something began to shift. I awoke in the morning and the ache was still there, but so was a little bit of energy. And the next week, the ache again but a little more energy.

I read about suicide—my brother had killed himself. I stumbled across words—in books, in magazines, from the mouths of friends and of strangers—that slowly, slowly began to envelop my numbness, to surround the ache, to melt the sorrow frozen inside. Through it all, I kept praying for comfort.

Someone said that God enters through our wounded areas. Quietly God began to enter my wounded areas, to cleanse the wounds and heal the pain. Slowly, quietly, comfort came.

I still miss my brother terribly. I still sometimes sob in my sleep when I dream about him. But the mourning melts into comfort. God is there—for me, for my brother. The pain is somehow blessed and made holy.

It is mysterious, sad, and wondrous beyond words.

When you face sorrow—the death of a friend, the loss of a love, the disappointment of a friendship, months when everything seems to go wrong—the promise remains. The promise is sure. "Blessed are those who mourn, for they will be comforted."

H.R.N.

# Strengthening Your Faith
## A Lover's Quarrel

Many people believe that the opposite of love is hate, but that's not true. Love's opposite is apathy—not caring.

Robert Frost, the legendary poet, understood that truth. He had these words engraved on his tombstone: "I had a lover's quarrel with the world." Frost's intensity of love for the world guaranteed that he would sometimes quarrel with it. That quarrel, for him, was evidence of his love.

A similar dynamic exists in your relationship to the faith. If you can get angry with God, agitated at the church, cynical about the faith, argumentative over Christianity's tradition, then you are a spiritual lover. Doubts and questions and quarrels signal a healthy faith. You're not in trouble when you doubt. You're only in trouble when you stop caring.

Perhaps you know people who always seems eager to

tangle over the faith, the church, things spiritual—people who are ready to ask the cynical question or to challenge traditional beliefs.

Don't be put off or fooled by such people. No matter how hard these "quarrelers" may try to put distance between themselves and the faith community, their emotional involvement betrays them. They are in reality spiritual lovers, caring so much about their relationship with God that they dare to argue with God.

Be patient with individuals like this. God uses time and reflection to heal these lovers' quarrels, and a stronger faith emerges because of them.

If you are the one having the lover's quarrel with God, be patient with yourself. God does find ways to transform such quarrels into foundations for a stronger faith.

Let your questions, doubts, and frustrations come. They reveal in you the lover, the fighter who will not let go. God can handle your honest feelings and your quarrels. God can take your hurts and disappointments and use them to strengthen your faith.

# FAITHFUL RELATIONSHIPS

## Keeping God at the Center

# INTERNAL AFFAIRS
## Caring for Your Body

You know the litany: Eat at least five fruits and vegetables a day. Drink plenty of water. Exercise three to five times a week. Avoid alcohol and other drugs. Get adequate rest. Keep a daily balance between work and play. It's called caring for your body. But ensuring proper care is a little trickier than you might think.

When the New Testament refers to body, it often uses the Greek word *soma*. The notion of *soma* encompasses the whole person—body, mind, emotions, will. In this New Testament way of understanding, it is impossible to separate body from soul. Each is inextricably bound up with the other.

Because your body and your spirit intertwine, caring for your body means not only eating right and exercising but also learning to listen to your body in a new way. If you can learn to listen to your body's wisdom, the body will give you signals about what kind of care it needs.

Richard Strozzi Heckler in *The Anatomy of Change: A Way to Move Through Life's Transitions* comments that we may know a lot about the nourishment that comes from proper diet and still remain ignorant about nourishment that comes from somewhere deep within us. We may know, for instance, that we need to jog for exercise and do so, but we can run miles every day and continue to be out of touch with what our body is telling us.

Caring for your body, then, means being connected with it, aware of feelings, sensations, and the messages it constantly sends you. Caring for your body means living through your body, not just in it.

Many of us are in touch—truly connected—with our body only when we get sick, fatigued, or stressed. In truth, it's often because we have ignored our body in the first place that we end up sick or tired.

In caring for your body, pay attention not only to what you put into it but also to what you expect out of it. Respect the wisdom of your body. The more in tune you are with how your body feels and the more you listen to your body, the more your body will be able to tell you what it needs.

You are wonderfully made. Care for your body. Respect its wisdom. Follow its leading.

# FRIENDSHIP

Many people will cross your path in the years ahead. They will influence you, and you in turn will have an influence on their lives. Some of these people will become your friends. Some of these friendships will last a lifetime.

Such friendships are important, but be very clear about one thing: Every friendship you start will go through many changes, some of them quite radical. Some friendships may even end. Yet each of us senses the need to seek, nurture, and value friendship, no matter what the risk. Given the benefits, friendship clearly merits that risk.

It takes commitment, trust, nurture, and adjustment for friendships to grow strong. *Commitment* implies being with someone for the long haul, through good times and bad. *Trust* includes the two-way street of having confidence in another person and being trustworthy yourself. *Nurture* calls for dedicating time and energy toward building a friendship. *Adjustment* describes the willingness to be flexible and open, accepting changes in your friendship and growing through those changes.

Most important of all, friendship requires *forgiveness*. Misunderstanding and hurt will occur in friendships, especially in friendships that are very close. Be ready to forgive. Be ready to ask for forgiveness for yourself. Be sensitive to the healing power forgiveness can bring to friendship, and be gracious with it.

Sadly, not all people are trustworthy. You will no doubt find yourself involved with some of those people, and you will be hurt when these "friendships" end. Even trustworthy lifelong friendships carry their share of disappointments. But the rich blessing of friendship gives life a depth of meaning unlike anything else. Ask God to guide you, be willing to spend time developing friendships, and the treasured shelter of a good friend will be yours.

# COPING WITH LONELINESS

Have you ever been lonely? Not just alone but downright lonely?

Loneliness happens to all of us at one time or another. Occasional loneliness at certain times just can't be avoided. That kind of loneliness—short-term, occasional—is the kind you wait out, knowing that it will end, knowing that the lonely feeling will go away.

Another kind of loneliness signals trouble of a different sort. This kind of loneliness finds you feeling lonely even when you are with a group of friends. This deep, pervasive loneliness causes you to push away the very people you care about. This loneliness builds and builds until you find yourself depressed and unwilling to make the effort to be with people.

When this kind of loneliness comes and stays, seek help. Talk with your minister or chaplain. Visit the student health center and talk with a counselor. Talk with a professor who seems approachable. Seek assistance in connecting with a caring community of Christians.

Pray and ask God to help you find people who can guide you through this difficult time. There are people out there who care, who are willing to help you.

When you come through to the other side of loneliness—and, with God's help, you will—remember how the healing came for you. Recall what facilitated your return to normalcy and make a list of those things. If loneliness comes around again, refer to that list. Or you may be able to share it with someone you know. It may be that you can help others who find themselves caught in that same downward spiral of loneliness.

Asking for help when you are lonely is the first step toward getting yourself—and perhaps someone else—through loneliness back to community. Share your feelings and let God use others to bring you to wholeness again.

# SEXUALITY
## God's Good Gift

Our sexuality is a good and great gift. With this gift comes an opportunity to relate to another person in a special way. The gift is different for each of us, yet our sexuality has many common threads.

This gift may hurt or heal, shatter or make whole, affirm or destroy. It is a gift of pleasure that may contribute to intimacy with another person. It is a gift that impacts us deeply—spiritually, psychologically, physically, emotionally, intellectually, ethically, and socially.

Sexuality can be a tremendous source of affirmation. It can provide a sense of security, physical safety, and joyful expectation. It can be part of a new creation. But to be honest, sexuality too often causes pain, abuse, confusion, injury, infection, even death.

Clearly God designed sexuality as an original blessing to us. Yet today sexual behavior seems overly affected by peer pressure and desires to belong. Engaging in sex casually may offer a temporary respite from loneliness. But the respite won't last; loneliness will return—perhaps accompanied by an eroding sense of self-esteem.

Sexuality may survive with little or no spiritual nurture, with casual use, or with careless choice. But sexuality thrives on careful discernment, spiritual affirmation, loving commitment, and a sense of awe and wonder. Those who use the gift of sexuality in the way God intended are willing to forego its promise of instant but shallow intimacy and seek to build a trusting, loving, and committed relationship as the foundation for healthy sexual expression.

We face numerous choices regarding our sexuality over the course of a lifetime. Many of those choices are difficult, complex, and have life-changing results. All around us are people willing to tell us how this gift can be used, should be used, must be used. Yet our knowledge that sexuality comes as a gift from God affects our decision making most dramatically. We must each pray through, think through, and talk through our decisions about this powerful gift for ourselves.

Scripture, tradition, reason, and your own experience—these are important sources for discovering what the gift of sexuality means to you. Ask for God's guidance; talk with someone whose life and faith you respect; don't substitute feelings for facts. Honor this great gift by seeking to know and understand its place in your life and in the lives of others.

May the gift of sexuality be a blessing in your life and a blessing to God, Creator of all gifts.

# YOUR SEXUALITY
## Making Choices with Integrity

~

It's a curious thing. If you do not think about and make plans for yourself, someone else certainly will. If you do not make decisions for yourself, plenty of others are more than willing to make decisions for you.

In some areas of your life, letting someone else decide might not be so bad. But we're talking about sexuality—your sexuality. Not your friends' sexuality. Not your roommate's. Not your parents'. Not your minister's. *Your* sexuality.

While sexuality is a tremendous gift from God, it can also be a source of pain, hurt, and abuse. Do you know that some of your peers in college were so sexually abused in childhood that their sense of self-worth has been eroded to a dangerously low level, severely damaging their ability to be physically affectionate?

Do you know that some of your peers are confused about their sexual orientation, paralyzed by shame, fear, and guilt, unsure of who they are sexually?

Do you know that others are so rigidly close-minded about their sexuality that their best approach to this gift from God is to label it "evil" and "sinful"?

Do you know that many refuse to take responsibility for their sexuality and engage in unprotected sexual activity, putting health and life at risk?

Do you know that there are some who believe the only way to express love for someone is to become sexually involved?

Do you know that some professors whom you respect are so confused about their sexuality that they may take advantage of your trust in order to exploit you sexually?

You must approach sexuality with much care, sensitivity, and discernment as you make decisions about how to live out your sexual life.

While you must make these decisions for yourself, you don't have to make them by yourself. Trusted friends, other believers in your faith community, words of guidance from scripture—these, along with prayer and reflection, can lead you to decisions that affirm your sexuality as the gift God intended.

# LIFE IN THE BALANCE
## Love and Relationships

Christianity and psychology stand on common ground in many areas. Perhaps the most important area of agreement is the place of love and relationship in our lives. All the mainline psychological theories agree that love and relationship are key elements for good mental health. Without loving relationships, a balanced life is at risk.

Whether you read Leviticus or Deuteronomy in the Hebrew scriptures or Matthew, Luke, Corinthians, or First John in the New Testament, you'll find that the Bible teaches the importance of loving relationships. God created each of us with a basic need to love and be loved. It is that simple. We all need the care and affection of others, and likewise we need to care for and about others.

You may not have noticed yet, but every relationship you

have changes as time goes by. Try as you might to keep your world neat and predictable, relationships change. In fact, the greater your emotional investment with someone, the more obvious the changes will be. The changes may not be easy, but they are necessary for a relationship to grow and survive.

So there it is: We all need loving relationships, and all relationships are guaranteed to change. But we do have some help in dealing with those realities. Jesus showed what God asks of us in relationships. We all have been blessed with a capacity to love with our heart, our soul, our mind, and our strength. God asks us to make our best effort to love with all our being.

We have a tremendous capacity to bless God by accepting God's love and loving God back with our heart, soul, mind, and strength. This kind of love makes the best foundation possible in other relationships as well.

Expect times when you will be hurt or your trust will be broken. Know even then that God yearns for loving relationships to fill your life. You can express your love by loving God back, loving others, and receiving others' love.

# LIFELONG RELATIONSHIPS

Approximately once every five years, on average, Americans change their address. The reasons for these moves vary—going to school, changing jobs, getting married or divorced, changes in health or financial status—but one result is sure: Such disruption radically affects our ability to develop and maintain lifelong relationships.

With this kind of mobility, most of us will be lucky to have four or five relationships that will last a lifetime. Count them any way you want—friend, spouse, relative—you probably will be able to number them on one hand. Given these statistics, developing and nurturing long-term relationships becomes a priority.

What is it that cements a relationship? What is it that enables people to stick with each other over the long haul?

What is it that finally makes or breaks a relationship? The key ingredient, it seems, is intimacy. That sounds simple enough until you start trying to define what it means. Is intimacy physical, financial, material? Does it come from shared interests, beliefs, values? Can intimacy be found in common hobbies, common likes, common dislikes?

The answer to all those questions turns out to be no. True intimacy—intimacy that will sustain a relationship over time—comes from the ability to resolve conflict. The ability to face disagreements and to reconcile is the key to whether two people will grow closer or will drift apart.

Imagine what a difference it would make in your relationships if you believed that no matter how deep the conflict, you and the person you love had a commitment to work out your differences—that the two of you would simply stay with it until the conflict was resolved. Together you would begin to build a foundation for intimacy unlike any other. You would develop a relationship of trust that would allow each of you to be yourself with the other. That kind of trust is an amazing gift to give another human being.

Jesus understood the significance of the commitment to resolve conflict. He believed that this ability, this willingness to stick to it, is so important that it even affects our relationship with God. In the Gospel of Matthew, Jesus says that we should make our offerings to God only after we have resolved our conflicts with others and have reconciled with them (Matt. 5:23-24).

The way to intimacy with another person—resolving conflict—also presents the way to intimacy with God. Just as you will have conflicts with those you love, so you also will have conflicts with God who loves you. When that happens, if you simply stay with it—through honest prayer and reflection—resolution will come, and you will experience the gift of intimacy with God.

Resolving conflict is the very stuff of intimacy, of trust, of relationships that last.

# BLESSED TO BE A BLESSING
## Sacrifice and Servant Leadership

In Hermann Hesse's story *The Journey to the East*, a band of men sets out on a mythical journey. The central figure, Leo, a servant, accompanies the party. He does menial chores for the men, but he also sustains them with his spirit and his song. He is, according to the story, a person of great spirit. When Leo disappears, the group falls into disarray, and the men abandon the journey.

The narrator, one of the band of men, after years of wandering, finds Leo and is taken into the secret society that had sponsored the journey. He discovers then that Leo, whom he had known first as a servant, was in fact the head of the order, its guiding spirit, a great and noble leader.

The idea of servant-leader is an old one. In the Bible, Jesus talks about how those who would be first will be last, and those who would be last will be first. Jesus himself, shortly before his death, picks up a towel and, acting as a servant, washes the feet of his disciples. The act shocks some of them, yet Jesus insists on washing each one's feet. It is a gift of service.

As Christians we are called to that same gift of service. Like the disciples, we must lose our lives in order to find them. We must give ourselves in order to understand who we truly are.

God blessed the ancient Hebrews with land, descendants, and possessions. At the same time, God made it clear that Israel was being blessed so that it, in turn, would be a blessing to others.

The gift of leadership is bestowed on people so that they may use it to bless others. Leading people is a holy task. You and I are blessed to be a blessing to others, and we lead by first serving.

# SOMEWHERE BETWEEN CRISIS AND OPPORTUNITY

## Life in the Wider World

# CHANGE
## Finding Your Way

"There will be moments when everything goes well; don't worry, it won't last." My favorite high school teacher offered that tongue-in-cheek advice when I went off to college. Unlike some of the other advice I received at the time, this observation later turned out to be true.

College always seemed to me to be something between crisis and opportunity. People eagerly told me that I would find myself on the growing edge of life, but they didn't tell me I would sometimes also find myself simply on the edge. They told me to be myself, but they didn't tell me there would be times when I didn't like the self I was being and when I would want to be someone else instead.

Change—in yourself, in your circumstances, and in your way of looking at things—is inevitable. Facing personal changes in the midst of a changing world can be painful. Going from what is comfortable and familiar to what is new and unfamiliar can sometimes be frightening. Moving through change is the process of living in the transition place between giving up the old and finding your place in the new.

You are not alone on this journey of change. Jim Henson, creator of the Muppets, considered life a process of growth. "I can't help but think of myself as a very 'human' being," he said. "I have the full complement of weaknesses, fears, problems, ego, sensuality, etc. But again, I think this is why we're here—to work our way through all this and to hopefully come out a bit wiser and better for having gone through it all."

Jesus, too, is your companion on this journey. The scriptures say that he experienced change. "And Jesus increased in wisdom and in years." As he moved through life, he met new circumstances, new relationships, new situations—challenges to change. It wasn't always easy for him; he wasn't always sure of himself.

The Bible itself tells the story of a people called to change. Abram and Sarai travel to a new country, with changed names to mark their journey. In the Hebrew scriptures, an encounter with God brings about profound personal and social change. In the New Testament, people's interactions with Jesus and his disciples results in changed lives.

Crisis. Opportunity. Change. All are inevitable on this journey called life. In the middle of the confusion and the chaos and the opportunity, try to remember that you are not alone. God—and some faithful fellow-journeyers—are with you through it all.

# MONEY
## Making Sense of It All

In ancient Egypt people were buried with their personal possessions and financial wealth because everyone assumed that these things would be helpful in the afterlife.

Tevye, the burdened father in the musical *Fiddler on the Roof* asked of God, "You made many, many poor people. I realize, of course, that it's no shame to be poor, but it's no great honor either. So what would have been so terrible if I had a small fortune?"

Jesus tells his disciples that it would be "easier for a camel to go through the eye of a needle than for someone who is rich to enter the kingdom of God" (Matt. 19:24).

At the same time that we note pockets of incredible greed in this country, we also discover that no country in the world surpasses the United States in charitable donations.

Money and our attitudes toward it are very confusing. Wending your way through the possibilities and the pitfalls surrounding money can be precarious. Maybe the following observations will help.

First, the drive to acquire money can become addictive. For some people, earning all the money they can becomes their number-one goal, and the costs are dear. As you set out to "earn a living," ask yourself this basic question: *What is my drive to acquire money costing me—in terms of relationships, career choice, physical and psychological health?*

Second, the balance between income and outgo affects your spirit. If you overextend your financial resources, you will find that every day holds worry about how much money you have, how much you need, and how to reconcile the difference between the two. The spiritual discipline of reducing your material needs results in much greater freedom when it comes to earning and managing money.

Third, what you do with your money matters. Giving away part of what you earn honors the biblical understanding that everything you have, including your ability to earn money, comes from God.

Finally, the amount of money you have can influence your relationship with God. In his public television special about the hymn "Amazing Grace," Bill Moyers interviews an elderly man who believes that having either too little or too much money makes it hard to experience God's grace—to appreciate the gospel's message of God's nurturing love for us and of our need for God's forgiveness. As you deal with money—whether out of extreme poverty, excessive riches, or somewhere in between—pay attention to its impact on your experience of God's grace.

# COPING WITH FAILURE

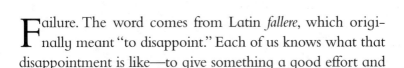

Failure. The word comes from Latin *fallere*, which originally meant "to disappoint." Each of us knows what that disappointment is like—to give something a good effort and to have that effort meet not with success but with failure.

The disappointment that comes with failure is bitter, and often you may be tempted to give up. Before you do, consider this: Dr. Seuss's book *And to Think That I Saw It on Mulberry Street* was rejected by twenty-three publishers before it was printed. *M\*A\*S\*H*, by Richard Hooker, was rejected twenty-one times. Richard Bach's *Jonathan Livingston Seagull* was published by the nineteenth publisher he approached. In addition to their perseverance in the face of failure, all three authors have something else in common: Each of their books was among the top best-sellers in the twentieth century.

The Bible cites numerous examples of people who faced failure but refused to give up. For many years, Sarah had been unable to conceive the child she and Abraham had been promised. In her old age, she gave birth to Isaac. Through him, Abraham and Sarah became the father and mother of a great people (Gen. 18:1-15; 21:1-7).

Peter, one of Jesus' disciples, faltered in his faith on a number of occasions over the course of his life—most notably on the night before the crucifixion, when he denied three times that he even knew Jesus (Luke 22:54-62). Yet Peter became the rock on which the church was built (Matt. 16:18).

Even Jesus experienced failure. Often the people who came to hear him misunderstood his message. When he preached in Nazareth, his hometown, people ran him out of town and tried to throw him off a cliff (Luke 4:16-30). Yet he too kept at it.

When you find yourself facing failure, take heart. As Samuel Johnson wrote, don't be ashamed of your failures. Instead, learn from them. Keep trying. Let your failures lead you to new paths. And remember, even though failure is an inevitable part of being human, it never has the final say in your life. God's grace is the final word. It is God's grace that picks you up when you fail. That same grace will carry you through whatever failures—of faith, of body, of mind—you come up against in the years ahead.

# FAITH AND POLITICS

In the summer of 1776, a committee including Thomas Jefferson as its chief contributor presented the document we know as the Declaration of Independence to the Continental Congress. Many hailed the declaration as a groundbreaking approach to individual rights and the political will.

One of the more famous lines from this document declared it "self-evident, that all men are created equal." But "men" included only free, property-owning males. Left out were slaves, women, and men without property.

From our vantage point today, to exclude these people from the political process would be abhorrent. Yet many faithful people involved in politics over the last two centuries have sought and fought to control what happens in our society by controlling who makes the decisions. Our "founding fathers" clearly were no different.

As you seek to participate in our democracy and as you exercise your Christian faith as a participant, consider these two observations:

1. Faith—even faith strong enough "to move mountains"—that is not based in love is at bottom "nothing" (1 Cor. 13:2).

2. A political stance—even a stance articulated with power and persuasion—that is not founded on justice for all people is at bottom morally bankrupt.

The interaction of love-based faith and justice-based politics promises dramatic transformation. Joining the two for social change demands continual focus on what Julia and Richard Wilke call, in the *Disciple Bible Study,* "the least, the last, and the lost." Ensuring basic levels of food, clothing, shelter, health care, and education for the least among us, the last among us, and the lost among us is the true measure of a society's greatness. Christians know the importance of this teaching, a teaching found throughout the Bible from Genesis to Revelation.

Faith and politics? Yes! Love and justice? Absolutely! These are all partners in making peace.

# DOING THE RIGHT THING
## Morality and Ethics

L ove the Lord your God with all your heart, mind, soul, and strength. Do justice. Give food to the hungry, and visit the imprisoned. Forgive and pray for your enemies.

These commands from the Bible seem straightforward enough. It's a simple matter of morality—knowing the difference between right and wrong and choosing the right. Jesus wants us to care for those who need care.

Yes, simple enough on paper, but getting down to living your daily life out of that biblical ethic can get confusing sometimes.

Here's an often cited scenario that challenges your ethical thinking. A woman's husband is terminally ill. One pharmaceutical drug could cure his disease and save his life, but the drug is still experimental, and the projected market value of the drug exceeds what the woman could possibly afford. Given the opportunity, should she steal the medication? Should her doctor mislead the insurance company so that it will cover the cost of the drug? Should the government sue the drug's patent owner and seize manufacture of the drug?

No easy answers exist in this dilemma. There are no simple choices to be made. Yet these decisions—like the ones human beings must make every day—are life-and-death decisions.

Balancing competing claims, working through all the implications of your position on an issue, being able to hear the truth in the argument of someone with whom you disagree—this is the stuff of morality. You must pay attention to all these dynamics in order to build an ethical foundation that is strong and consistent—one that will empower you to "do the right thing."

It's not easy, but God calls us to the struggle; and the struggle is worth it.

# SUFFERING AND EVIL

G*od is good. God is just. God is all-powerful.* You can reconcile any two of these statements, someone once said;
but you cannot reconcile all three.

Evil, suffering, death. It's not necessary to have lived Job's
life to understand how bad life can be—the unhelpable bad-
ness of the world. Suffering and evil are sometimes overwhelming forces in our lives.

What do you say to a parent whose child has died? What
do you feel when you hear of "ethnic cleansing" in Eastern
Europe? What can you do as you look into the face of
the terror and brutality of the September 11 attacks in
New York, Washington, and that Pennsylvania field? What
do feel when you read about the horrors of the Holocaust?
How do you face the death of someone you love?

You begin perhaps by facing such events with rage and anger. You challenge God. You call God to account. The psalmist is not afraid to say it: "Why do you cast me off? Why do you hide your face from me?" (Ps. 88:14).

This rage and questioning does not diminish God; quite the opposite—it takes God seriously. As Elie Wiesel says, "I do not have any answers, but I have some very good questions."

Job is sure that God has deprived him of justice in his life, but he swears that as long as he is alive, he will not give up his faith in God. Job stakes out a difficult position, one that generations of Jewish and Christian believers follow: Job will believe but not without question. As Rabbi David Wolpe writes in *The Healer of Shattered Hearts*, "Protest does not answer the question of evil, but it helps maintain the sanity of the accuser."

Inherent in our faith is another truth about suffering. And while this truth doesn't provide an answer to the question of evil, it is a powerful companion to us in the midst of that evil. That truth is our belief that no injustice in this world is suffered alone. No abuse is suffered alone. No evil is suffered alone. No death is suffered alone.

Where was God when the Jews were in the concentration camps on their way to the death chambers? God was in the camps on the way to the death chambers.

God suffers with us. God weeps with us. God dies with us.

The suffering of God is powerful. It witnesses to God's intimacy with us. It matters that when we suffer, we do not suffer alone. It matters very much.

But companionship does not cure pain, and God's suffering with us, as powerful as it is, cannot be an answer to the ravages of evil. Ultimately no answer satisfies. Some attempts at answers are helpful. Some get us through one day to the next. But in the end, answers elude our grasp. The answer, according to Rabbi Yannai, a classic Jewish scholar, is not in our hands. In this life, that may be the last word: "It is not in our hands."

So we continue to weep. We continue to rage. We continue to suffer with others. And we continue to pray.

# PEACEMAKING IN A VIOLENT WORLD

Richard Rhodes, winner of the Pulitzer Prize for his book *The Making of the Atomic Bomb*, lost his mother to suicide when he was thirteen months old. It was the middle of the Depression. When he was ten, his father remarried. Richard's stepmother turned out to be as cruel as the worst of folklore-cruel stepmothers.

For two and a half years, Richard and his brother were abused—kicked, beaten, denied baths and showers, deliberately starved. In *A Hole in the World: An American Boyhood*, he writes, "I've often wondered how my brother and I survived with our capacity to love intact. I always come back to the same answer—strangers helped us."

In the face of cruelty, poverty, and abuse, strangers helped the two boys. Rhodes goes on to explain that doing nothing allows evil to happen. "Don't be a bystander," he says. "Do something."

*Do something.* In the Hebrew tradition, this is called *tikun olam*—the repair, the healing of the world. It is peacemaking. That may seem a tall order—to make peace, to repair the world—especially after the September 11 attacks. And it is a tall order. But God calls you each and every day to be a peacemaker, a healer, a repairer.

There are so many ways—little and big—to do that. The sensitivities, the skills, and the time with which God has graced you will present many chances to do the things that make for peace. One day at a time. One small corner of the world at a time. One piece at a time. One peace at a time.

# LOVE YOUR MOTHER
## You and the Planet

These are the overwhelming facts:

- The earth loses rain forests at the rate of one football field a second.
- There is no "away" when you throw something away.
- Anthrax and other biological weapons threaten the world as never before.
- One hundred of the world's five to ten million species become extinct every day.

There is no doubt about it: We have placed the earth in great danger. Surely this is not what God intended when, according to the scriptures, God gave humanity dominion over creation. Surely Adam did not name the creatures of the world so that we might kill them off one species at a time.

But what to do? Start simply. That is what the Quakers would have you do. Answer for yourself some questions the Quakers ask:

- Am I walking gently on the earth? What are some ways I can live more simply, mindful of how my life affects the earth and its resources?

- Do I honor the life of all living things? Do I seek the holiness that God has placed in these things and the measure of light that God has lent them?

- What actions am I taking to reverse the destruction of the earth's ecosystems and to promote her healing?

- Do I recognize that the preparation for and the conduct of war are among the greatest causes of environmental degradation?

- Does my daily life exemplify and reflect my respect for the oneness of creation and my care for the environment?

- Do I examine and appreciate cultures and communities whose lives are based on close harmony with the natural world?

Start simply. Turn off the faucet while you brush your teeth. Bundle newspapers for recycling. Recycle plastic, cardboard, cans. If you're able, use stairs instead of the elevator. Even simple things make a difference. Love your Mother. Walk gently on the earth.

# Reaching beyond Yourself

In the middle of class schedules, work, close relationships, and play, be sure to include time for "reaching beyond yourself." Finding the energy and interest to become involved in other people's lives maintains good mental and spiritual health.

Throughout the Bible we find examples of the call to serve others. Helping, caring for, and loving others blesses God and is a fitting response to God's love.

Methodism's founder, John Wesley, believed and taught that "good works" naturally spring from our faith in Jesus Christ. Wesley felt these deeds would benefit not only the ones served but also the ones who served. In fact, many counselors today will tell you that simply reaching out and caring for another is a helpful treatment for depression.

Perhaps you could reach beyond yourself and just listen to someone who is hurting physically or spiritually. Or you could become involved in a group that seeks to meet some of the emotional and physical needs of others. Find out what your campus ministry or local church does to help others and link up with a program. Consider joining a mission work team over spring break. Lots of organizations need your volunteer time as you seek to reach out.

Clearly Jesus taught us that whoever is in need is our neighbor, the neighbor we are called to love.

# ABOUT THE AUTHORS

TOM ETTINGER AND HELEN NEINAST, former campus ministers at Emory University in Atlanta, are currently writers who live in the mountains of northeast Georgia. They offer retreats for older youth, for college students, and for young adults. Previously Tom served campus ministries and pastorates in the Florida Conference of The United Methodist Church and maintained a private counseling practice. Helen was director of the Division of Higher Education at the Board of Higher Education and Ministry of The United Methodist Church.

Tom is a graduate of University of South Florida and earned the M.Div. from Duke University Divinity School. Helen is a graduate of McMurry University in Abilene, Texas, and also earned an M.Div. from Duke. Both Tom and Helen earned the Doctor of Ministry in spiritual formation from Graduate Theological Foundation in Indiana.

# DISCOVER YOURSELF, YOUR PATH, YOUR WORLD, YOUR GOD.

By definition MethodX means "the way of Christ." By application it invites you to identify and explore your relationship with God and the world around you. Filled with humor, prayer methods, scripture, and more, MethodX addresses from a Christian perspective the many issues young adults face daily.

**www.methodx.net—the way of Christ**
An online community for young adults.